HOW TO NOT DIE ALONE

LOVE THAT LASTS

You Deserve To Be Happy

Arya Taylor

Table of Contents

PART 1 5
Chapter 1: 6 Signs You May Be Lonely 6
Chapter 2: 9 Tips on How To Have A Strong Relationship 10
Chapter 3: *9 Ways to Achieve Harmony In Your Professional Relationships* ... 17
Chapter 4: *6 Signs You Have A Fear of Intimacy* 22
Chapter 5: *How To Be Your Own Best friend* 26
Chapter 6: *8 Signs You Have Found Your Soulmate* 29
Chapter 7: *6 Steps To Recover From A Breakup* 34
Chapter 8: *6 Dating Red Flags To Avoid* 38
Chapter 9: *6 Tips To Have A Healthy Long-Distance Relationship* ... 42
PART 2 46
Chapter 1: 10 Signs You're Falling In Love 47
Chapter 2: How To Survive a Long Distance Relationship 53
Chapter 3: What To Do When Your Partner Cheats On You 59
Chapter 4: *6 Relationship Goals To Have* 62
Chapter 5: *What Happens When You Get Bored In A Relationship* ... 66
Chapter 6: *Feeling Insecure In Your Relationship* 69
Chapter 7: *7 Signs You Have Found A Keeper* 72
Chapter 8: *6 Behaviours That Keep You Single* 76
Chapter 9: 9 Signs of a Toxic Relationship 80
PART 3 85
Chapter 1: 7 Reasons Why Men Cheat 86
Chapter 2: *6 Ways To Flirt With Someone* 90
Chapter 3: *6 Ways To Deal With Betrayal* 94
Chapter 4: *6 Ways To Be More Confident In Bed* 98
Chapter 5: *6 Tips To Find The One* 102
Chapter 6: *6 Signs You Have Found A Real Friend* 106
Chapter 7: *6 Signs You Are Emotionally Unavailable* 109

Chapter 8:   *6 Lessons You Can Learn From A Breakup*............................ 113
Chapter 9:   *6 Signs Your Love Is One Sided*... 117

PART 1

Chapter 1:
6 Signs You May Be Lonely

What is that one emotion that leads us to anxiety, depression, or stress? People often feel this emotion when they have no one around to support them. That is being lonely. What is being lonely? "When one is unable to find life's meaning," or simply put, it is the feeling of isolation. You often find yourself in a corner then outside with friends or family. Sometimes, these emotions are triggered by discouragement by close ones and negativity of life. We try to bear it alone rather than risking the judgment of others. We try to hide it as much as possible. Then, eventually, it becomes a habit. Then even if it's news worth sharing, we keep it to ourselves.

Loneliness can drive a person to harm themselves, either physically or mentally, or both too. It can change our lives drastically. Going out seems to be a burden. It feels tiresome even to move an inch. So, we tend to stay in one place, probably alone. But it doesn't always mean that you are feeling sad. Sometimes you feel happy being alone. It all depends on how you look at things.

1. **Feeling Insecure**

When we look around us, we see people every day. This type of connection with people can lead to two conclusions. Positive or negative.

A positive attitude may lead to appreciation. However, negative emotions will lead to insecurities. This insecurity will lead us to go out as little as possible. And whatever we hate about us, we feel it more prominent. Eventually, we never go out at all. Because of the fear that people might judge us at our worst trait. We think that even our family is against us, which makes it even more difficult.

2. Anger Becomes A Comrade

It becomes hard to express what we feel to others. When we feel like there is no one we can genuinely tell our feeling to, they bottle up. We start to bottle up our emotions to don't get a chance to tell others about them. And those bottle-up emotions turn into anger the most easily. Even the slightest thing could make us aggressive. We get angry over all petty stuff, and gradually, it becomes our release to all the emotion. It becomes easier to show your anger than other emotions.

3. It Starts To Hurt Us Physically

Stress is one of the feelings you get out of being lonely. It is only natural that you stress about everything when you are alone in a situation. Scientifically, it is proven that staying alone most of the time raises our stress hormone, and it becomes a heart problem in the future. Most of us have experienced the tightening of our chest at times. That is when our stress hormone raises it builds up around our heart. It may also result in inflammation and some vascular problems. So, being lonely all the time may be physically harmful to us, and we should take it seriously.

4. Highly Harmful To Mental Health

Mental health is just as important as physical health. We need to focus on both equally. Loneliness can be harmful to our mental health in many ways. It often leads to hallucinations. It causes depression and anxiety. These types of mental occurrences are proven fatal if not dealt with immediately. It also drives us to overthink, which is equally as harmful as others. Isolation keeps your brain in a constant phase of resentment.

5. Lack Of Hope and Self-Compassion

Getting lonely sometimes is okay. It gets serious when you do not want to let go of it. When there is no hope, it feels like there is no reason to return—staying alone forces you into feeling empty and unwanted, thus, losing hope of ever being wanted again. Because discouragement surrounds us, we feel safe staying alone most of the time. We lose all the passion we once had, and it makes us dull. Things that once we loved doing feel like a burden. Gradually, we become addicted.

6. Negativity

Positivity and negativity are two aspects of daily life. And in life, when loneliness is our companion, we choose negativity to go through our day. Everything seems to be too much work, and everything in life seems dark. Negativity is the only thing we keep because it looks more suitable to lonely people. It causes emotional harm to people and tends to get in the way of an average daily routine. However, the negative side is what we choose every day.

Conclusion

We can feel lonely even after being surrounded by people because it's just something people feel in themselves. They don't realize that there are people who are willing to talk to them. Being lonely can cause one a lot of harm and disrupt all the day's work. But it doesn't always mean that lonely people are unhappy. Loneliness can bring peace too.

Chapter 2:
9 Tips on How To Have
A Strong Relationship

Who doesn't want a strong relationship? Everyone wants to have that high-level understanding with their partner that lasts a lifetime. It is scientifically proven that people who are in healthy relationships have less stress and more happiness.

Healthy relationship not only helps us increase our overall feelings of happiness, but stress-reduction also helps us improve our overall quality of physical and mental health that make every-day life more pleasing to go through. Relationships can be in the form of family, work, friendships, and also romantic ones. Depending on the area that matters the most to you at this very point in your life, you can choose to focus on that specific one until you feel you are ready to focus on the next.

If building powerful relationships is a priority of yours as it is mine, then stay with me till the end of this video because we will be discussing **9 Magical** Tips on How To Have A Strong Relationship with whoever you want. Let's Begin.

Number one
Listen to Each Other

This is the first and probably the most important thing that you might want to take note of. Just think, how many arguments have you had that went in the wrong direction just because no one was willing to simply just listen? In order to understand each other's point of view both parties must be willing to open up their ears instead of their mouths first. You need to have the stamina to listen to their side of the story before airing yours.

If you truly want a healthy relationship then the foundations starts with a good listening ear. To listen not only when the other party have problems in their lives, but also when they have a problem with you. Develop a good sense of compassion and empathy in the process.

Bitter thoughts, grudge-holding, and negativity toward the other person only serve to weaken your relationships, not strengthen them. So try to understand each other, let the other person speak, and then sort things out in the best possible way.

Number two
Give Time For The Relationship To Grow

For any relationship to truly blossom, it is important to spend the necessary quality time together. Whether the relationship is with family members, friends, or lovers, it takes energy and effort nonetheless. Any amount of energy you spend on that person will reap its benefits later.

Now, I am not saying to drastically change your life or to go on adventures or expensive dates to make your relationship healthy. All you have to do is simply get yourself free for a day or night once a week and do something different together, like having a date night, playing games, cooking and eating, watching movies or whatever you like, just give your best at that time. Be present with them and don't be distracted checking your phone or replying work messages.

Number three
Give Time To Yourself

Now I needed to talk about this one right after the number two. I think a good relationship should be balanced. In the previous point, I talked about spending quality time in relationships, but I also don't mean that you should give all your energy to them or stop doing things that energizes your soul. Don't sacrifice your own hobbies for the sake of others. I agree that you need to take more initiative in relationships but at the same time you need to take care of your own happiness too. So give time to yourself and spend it doing things that fills your soul with happiness and gratefulness. You will feel recharged and fresh as a result when you engage in your relationships.

Number four
Learn To Appreciate Little Things

This point will touch more on the romantic relationship side of things. If you are in a relationship for quite a while then there is a chance that you might get complacent and too comfortable. You might also gradually forget the little things that make the person special. As a result the other person could potentially feel like you may be taking them for granted. To avoid this, you need to start making it a constant reminder to yourself to appreciate the little things your partner does for you. Say "I love you" to them, give cute little gifts, give them surprises and tell them how much they mean to you. You need to show your partner how much you love them so they never feel taken for granted. So yeah, start doing all this and make your bond strong!!

Number five
Learn To Forgive

It is well said, "relationships require a lot of forgiveness". As I mentioned earlier, bitter thoughts and grudge-holding just hurt your relationship in the long run. So if you want a happy relationship then you should learn to forgive. If there is something on your mind that your partner did and you can't forget then sit and talk to them about it and try to come up with a good solution. If any of you makes any mistake, you should forgive them with a smiling face and tell them that these little mistakes can't lessen your love. Work on yourself, make your heart ready for what you see coming and even what you don't see coming, and let things go in the right direction. You need to make your heart learn to forgive, this is the only key.

Number Six
Don't expect your partner to complete you

You should be confident about whatever you have. If you are looking for a healthy relationship then you should not expect your partner to complete you. Sometimes, we expect things from our partners which we lack and it can put a strain on your relationship. What you could do instead is to constantly work on yourself to the point that you feel you truly and rightfully deserving of every good thing that comes your way. That you feel secure and independent at the same time in the relationship. Loving yourself first goes a long way in maintaining a strong and healthy relationship with others.

Number Seven
Ways Of Showing Love

Different people show and receive love in their own unique ways. Understanding how the other party expresses or receives love is the key to building a strong relationship. Some people do it by caring for you while others express it through physical affection like hugs and kisses. If you don't know that the specific love language is between you and the other party then it might cause problems in the long run. To really ensure the other party feels loved you have to express it in the way that they receive the most strongly. Go find out what they are by asking them and then start giving it right away!

Number eight
Be Flexible

If you want a healthy relationship then you have to learn to be flexible as well. Flexible in the face of any changes that might occur in your relationship. It is a known fact that change is the only constant in life. We may never be prepared but we should do our best to adapt to new situations that we may find ourselves in. It is also therefore unrealistic not to expect our relationships to change as time progresses as well. Learn to adapt and grow in this new stage and you will be all the more happier for it.

Number nine
Make Decisions Jointly

A good and healthy relationship requires listening to each others' desires and concerns. While you may not always love to do the things that the other party wants, you should always try to find a compromise that suits both of your needs. Instead of insisting and making decisions all the time, try making decisions together that both of you will find enjoyable. Be it where to hang out, what to eat for a meal, where to go on a trip together, or even what kinds of products to buy for your home, make sure that the other party's points of view is heard so that they don't end up resenting you over the long run.

Chapter 3:
9 Ways to Achieve Harmony In Your Professional Relationships

Offices are a microcosm of humanity. They are a mix of all types of people, with all types of personalities, quirks, goals, and challenges, so for everyone to get along beautifully, it takes effort.

You probably remember a time in your career when a "clash of personalities" corrupted a productive working environment. You can prevent this from happening and create harmony in your office with these nine simple practices.

1. Say Thank You

These two little words may be the most powerful when it comes to creating happiness and harmony. People work hard and take pride in their accomplishments but can feel overlooked. Taking time to acknowledge even the smallest achievement can make a person feel valued. Say thank you not only for the big job they've completed, say thank you when they open the door, offer to get you coffee or invite you to lunch. Offer a genuine thank you every day.

2. Notice The Little Things

If a co-worker or employee is happy at their job, they will go out of their way to add a little extra to their commitment. They might take on an extra assignment or stay late to help out with an uncompleted project. Or they may do subtle things like clean up the kitchen area or edit a company document on which they noticed errors. The more you notice and offer thanks for these little "extras," the more you will build happiness and harmony in the office, and the more motivated your co-workers will become to continue looking for ways to improve the business.

3. Avoid Idle Gossip

Gossip can tarnish office harmony. It might seem entertaining at the moment, but underneath, it builds distrust. Resentments build, people begin to wonder if they are the ones being gossiped about, and chasms open. Establish a "no-gossip policy" and enforce it. Extend your no-gossip policy for events outside the office as well, such as happy hours, company outings, or holiday parties, where relaxed environments and alcohol can loosen inhibitions.

4. Maintain An Open-Door Policy

Establish an open environment for discussion by creating a "come to me anytime" system. Be open to suggestions, complaints, or discussions without judgment. Because people come from different backgrounds and experiences, everyone has their way of looking at things. By listening, you can understand what others see from their point of view instead of your own. When people feel open to talk, you can nip problems in the bud before they escalate into real obstacles or unearth substantial opportunities you may not have noticed before.

5. Create A Team Environment

Hold regular meetings with the entire office and empower co-workers to take "ownership" of the business. If they feel their opinions and insights hold value, they will be more likely to use their talents and creativity to help build the business as a whole. Instead of taking orders, they will work together to look for ways to improve.

6. Offer To Help

Jump in and be hands-on yourself. Whenever you are stuck, overworked, or faced with a major deadline, you know how you appreciate a helping hand. It may take a little extra effort, but pitch in to help your co-workers over a hump.

7. Socialize Outside Of Work

Build friendships and harmonies outside of work with casual outings. Plan a monthly happy hour, establish a yearly barbeque picnic or kick up a friendly competition with a bowling or softball tournament. The relaxed environment will create bonds that go deeper than the company's latest accounting policies.

8. Get Everyone Involved

Every employee likes to be informed and in the loop, even if the news has nothing to do with them. Keeping an employee informed is an effortless way to make them feel appreciated and valuable in your business. Beyond this, you should always trust your team and be confident in delegating work to them – nobody likes working under a boss who micromanages everything they do and gives them no individuality in their work. Getting everyone involved is an easy way to please even the lowest-level employees and ensure that your office has harmony.

9. Communicate

Communication is crucial for any work environment. Every boss needs to have an open-door policy and be willing to talk to an employee at any time; on the other hand, every employee needs to be sure that they reach out and talk to higher-level employees. Learning is crucial in any office, and the central way for workers to learn is through communication. Beyond communication about work, occasional non-work-related talk is also important – it's a bad sign if you don't know anything about your fellow worker outside of work. Ask someone about their family or hobbies or whatever it may be; these small talk conversations may seem meaningless but are important for building harmony in the workplace.

Chapter 4:
6 Signs You Have A Fear of Intimacy

Intimacy avoidance or avoidance anxiety, also sometimes referred to as the fear of intimacy, is characterized as the fear of sharing a close emotional or physical relationship with someone. People who experience it do not consciously want to avoid intimacy; they even long for closeness, but they frequently push others away and may even sabotage relationships for many reasons.

The fear of intimacy is separate from the fear of vulnerability, though both of them can be closely intertwined. A person who has a fear of intimacy may be comfortable becoming vulnerable and showing their true self to their trusted friends and relatives. This problem often begins when a person finds relationships becoming too close or intimate. Fear of intimacy can stem from several causes. Overcoming this fear and anxiety can take time, but you can work on it if you know the signs of why you have the fear in the first place.

1. Fear Of Commitment

A person who has a fear of intimacy can interact well with others initially. It's when the relationship and its value grow closer that everything starts to fall apart. Instead of connecting with your partner on an intimate level, you find ways and excuses to end the relationship and replace it with yet another superficial relationship. Some might even call you a 'serial dater,' as you tend to lose interest after a few dates and abruptly end the relationship. The pattern of emerging short-term relationships and having a 'commitment phobia' can signify that you fear intimacy.

2. Perfectionism

The idea of perfectionism often works to push others away rather than draw them near. The underlying fear of intimacy often lies in a person who thinks he does not deserve to be loved and supported. The constant need for someone to prove themselves to be perfect and lovable can cause people to drift apart from them. Absolute perfectionism lies in being imperfect. We should be able to accept the flaws of others and should expect them to do the same for us. There's no beauty in trying to be perfect when we know we cannot achieve it.

3. Difficulty Expressing Needs

A person who has a fear of intimacy may have significant difficulty in expressing needs and wishes. This may stem from feeling undeserving of another's support. You need to understand that people cannot simply 'mind read,' they cannot know your needs by just looking at you; this might cause you to think that your needs go unfulfilled and your feelings of unworthiness are confirmed. This can lead to a vicious cycle of you not being vocal about your needs and lacking trust in your partner, and your relationship is meant to doom sooner or later.

4. Sabotaging Relationships

People who have a fear of intimacy may sabotage their relationship in many ways. You might get insecure, act suspicious, and accuse your partner of something that hasn't actually occurred. It can also take the form of nitpicking and being very critical of a partner. Your trust in your partner would lack day by day, and you would find yourself drifting apart from them.

5. Difficulties with Physical Contact

Fear of intimacy can lead to extremes when it comes to physical contact. It would swing between having a constant need for physical contact or avoiding it entirely. You might be inattentive to your partner's needs and solely concentrate on your own need for sexual release or gratification. People with a fear of intimacy may also recoil from sex altogether. Both ends of the spectrum lead to an inability to let go or communicate intimately emotionally. Letting yourself be emotionally naked and bringing up your fears and insecurities to your partner may help you overcome this problem.

6. You're Angry - A Lot

One way that the deep, subconscious fear of intimacy can manifest is via anger. Constant explosions of anger might indicate immaturity, and immature people are not able to form intimate relationships. Everyone gets angry sometimes, and it's an emotion that we cannot ignore, even if we want to. But if you find that your feelings of anger bubble up constantly or inappropriately, a fear of intimacy may be lurking underneath. Don't deny these intimacy issues, but instead put them on the table and communicate effectively with the person you are interested in.

Conclusion

Actions that root out in fear of intimacy only perpetuate the concern. With effort, especially a good therapist, many people have overcome this fear and developed the understanding and tools needed to create a long-term intimate relationship.

Chapter 5:
How To Be Your Own Best friend

Why would you want to become your own best friend? There are several benefits to creating your internal support system rather than relying on your partner, friends, or family to be there for you when you're suffering. Having other people's expectations can lead to disappointment, heartbreak, and relationship breakdown if your expectations aren't met.

We all have it in us to give ourselves what we need without seeking it externally.

Of course, it's great if you have a strong support network, but you could still benefit from becoming more self-reliant. And what about if you have no one to turn to for help, or if your current support people are unable to be there for you?

Isn't it far better to know how to support yourself in times of need? Here's how to become your own best friend.

1. Be Nice To Yourself

The first step to becoming a friend is to treat yourself like you would treat a friend. That means that you need to stop being self-critical and beating yourself up. Start by acknowledging your good qualities, talents, and abilities and begin to appreciate your unique self.

When you catch yourself thinking up some nasty self-talk, stop and ask, "Would I say this to my best friend?" If not, then reframe your self-talk to be more supportive and caring.

2. Imagine How You Would Support A Friend In The Same Situation

Think about a loved one, a friend, a family member, someone dear to you and imagine that they are in the same situation you are currently facing. Think about how they're struggling, suffering, and feeling stuck with this problem, then consider how to best offer assistance and advice to them.

Craft the words that you would say to your greatest friend and then say them gently to yourself. Allow yourself to feel supported, and give yourself what you need.

3. Honor Your Needs

Following the theme of considering how you would help a dear friend, **you need to start taking your advice and putting your own needs first**. Do you need a day off from work? A long hot bath? An early night? A wild night? Some time to catch up on your reading, cleaning, gardening, creative projects, social life, or self-care?

Whatever you need, allow yourself to **put it at the top of the list rather than the bottom**. Be there for yourself and make it happen.

4. Send Compassion To The Part of You That is Hurting

Being a friend to yourself involves adopting and mastering the art of self-compassion. Compassion isn't forceful or solution-focused. **Compassion is accepting, peaceful, and loving, without the need to control or change anything.**

Imagine a mother holding a child who has bumped his head. Her compassion is a strong force. She simply holds her child with loving, comforting, gentle arms and whispers, "It will be alright, my love." The child trusts his mother's words just as you learn to trust your own words when speaking to yourself.

Imagine yourself as both the child and the mother simultaneously. Offer compassion at the same time as you open up to receive it.

Use these techniques to become your own best friend and start *being there* **for yourself!**

Chapter 6:
8 Signs You Have Found Your Soulmate

"People think a soulmate is your perfect fit, and that's what everyone wants. But a true soulmate is a mirror, the person who shows you everything that is holding you back, the person who brings you to your attention so you can change your life." - Elizabeth Gilbert.

Legends say that even before you were born, the name of your spiritual half was determined. The two souls roam around the world to find their significant other. Whenever they find one another, they will unite, and their spirits would become one. But finding our long-lost soulmate isn't as easy as we think it is. Out of 7 billion people, it could take some time to find out our perfect match. However, when we meet them, we'll click with them instantly and just know in our hearts that they are made for us. A soulmate is someone you keep coming back to, no matter the struggles, challenges, obstacles, downfalls, or any of the circumstances. Everything would feel perfect with them. But how do you know if someone is your soulmate? You needn't worry! We have compiled for you below the signs that you may have found your soulmate.

1. **They would bring the best in you:**

Have your friends called you boring or a party pooper since you have entered adult life? Of course, you blame it all on the fact that you have grown up now and have responsibilities. But there's this one person who tends to bring out the fun and sassy side of yours. You feel so comfortable around them that you're even willing to try new things with them. They make your anxiety and fear go away in the blink of an eye. Be it singing songs loudly in the crowd, trying bungee jumping, or just packing up your bags and moving across the country with them to pursue your goals and dreams, they will strengthen you by supporting your decisions and being there for you.

2. They won't play games with you:

They won't be inconsistent with you, like making you feel special one day and ignoring you completely the next. You won't be questioning his feelings about you or putting yourself in a state of over-thinking. Sure, they won't make grand gestures like showing up at your window holding a guitar at 3 in the morning or putting up a billboard saying how much they love you (although we will happily accept both). Still, they will make you realize your worth in their life by always prioritizing you, making you happy, asking about you throughout the day, and paying close attention to whatever you say.

3. You respect each other's differences:

When starting a new relationship, people tend to avoid or hold back specific thoughts, beliefs, or opinions. This is because, in the game of love, both of the couple's emotions are at stake. They don't speak their mind until and unless they're entirely comfortable with their partner. Your soulmate would always be open to change and respect your opinions and views, even if they disagree. They wouldn't ever implement their beliefs and ideas on you but would instead find comfort in knowing that you both don't have the same set of minds. It's essential to be on the same page with your partner on certain things, like the future, life goals, children, etc., but it's okay to have different moral and political views, as long as you both respect each other and it doesn't hurt the other's sentiments.

4. You forgive each other:

Being soulmates doesn't save you from the wrath of arguments and fights. Every relationship experiences indifference and frustration from time to time. But it is one of the things that makes your bond stronger with your partner. You both would rather sit and try to talk it through or sort it out instead of going to bed angry at each other. And when it comes to forgiving the other, you both would do it in a heartbeat. You wouldn't consider holding the other person guilty and would make unique gestures to try and make it up with them.

5. You give each other space:

Your partner doesn't constantly bug you by texting and calling you every minute. They don't ask you about your whereabouts and don't act overly possessive. And rightly so, you do the same with them. You give each other your space and know that the other person would always be there for you. Even if you have to ask them about some distance, they respect it without complaining. You both trust each other with your whole heart and respect them enough to give them the space they have asked for.

6. You empathize with each other:

If your soulmate tells you about them getting good grades in college, finding their dream job, or getting a promotion, you find yourself being more excited and happier for them than they are. Sometimes, we feel drained out by showing too much empathy to other people and understanding and friendly. But with your soulmate, you don't have to force it out or pretend, and it just comes naturally. Whenever they feel scared or anxious, you're right there with them, protecting them from the world and not leaving their side until you make sure they're okay.

7. You communicate with each other effectively:

They say that communication is essential for any long-lasting relationship. If you aren't communicating well with your partner, you might find yourself in the depths of overthinking the worst-case scenarios. Your partner makes it easy for you to share with them, even if you hadn't done the deed before. You find yourself talking about the tough things, the things that bother you or hurt you, and they comfort and console you reassure you that they will fix it. Similarly, you make sure your partner speaks your mind to you, and you do your best to right your wrongs and clear any of their doubts.

8. You have seen each other's flaws and still loves each other the same:

It isn't easy to accept someone with the habits or traits that you despise. However, you have been your complete and utter authentic version of yourself with them, and they still love you the same. Be it crying loudly while watching an emotional sitcom, binge eating at night, snoring, burping, or just showing them your weak and vulnerable phase when you tend to push everyone away and dress up like a homeless drug addict. They find your quirks cute and accept you with all your imperfections and flaws, and you do the same with them.

Conclusion:

A soulmate is someone who makes you realize your worth and brings out the best in you. They might drive you crazy, ignites your triggers, stirs your passions, but they might also be your most excellent teacher. They would allow you to discover your true self while always being there for you and supporting you all the way.

Chapter 7:
6 Steps To Recover From A Breakup

Breakups are tough to go through. Even when they end with good terms, it still brings out many insecurities and traumas of the past. These include the fear of abandonment, loneliness, etc. Breakups have become a prevalent thing for us, so familiar that we sometimes forget how painful it can be. When you have imagined your whole future with someone, and someone ends up leaving you, you feel broken, but you would know it happened for a reason. Recovering from a breakup is not an impossible thing to do, and most of us recover from a partition even if it may take some time. Here are a few steps to recover from a breakup.

1. **Talk About It**

After a breakup, everything seems to be falling apart, and it is tough to talk about it, about the pain it has caused. But it is scientifically proven that talking about your breakup helps you recover from it; as you start talking about it, you are reminded about what went wrong. This enables you to understand that it was for good. When you talk about it to others, they tell you their perspective, and you start to see things from a different point of view; this way, you understand what went wrong, and you begin to feel more okay with things.

2. Keep A Journal

Even though talking helps, sometimes we can't find the right person to talk to, who will understand us. In a situation like this, you can always start journaling; it is an emotional release, where you write about your feelings, where you pour your heart out. You will feel more comfortable because no one will judge you; as you start writing, your hands would automatically write something that would surprise you, but those surprising things will help you figure yourself out.

3. Write Again and Again

When journaling, act as if you are telling all these things to a stranger and don't stop just then, write again and again as if you are talking to a different stranger every time you write about your breakup, it will help you gain a different perspective, you would realize many things, but above all, you would learn that whatever happened, happened for a better tomorrow.

4. Let It All Out

When going through a breakup, we all want to scream, shout and let all the anger out, but of course, you can't do all these things in public. So take some time out for yourself, go somewhere private, and talk all the anger, frustration, and tears out. It is normal to feel this way after a breakup, but remember that bottling up your emotions is never good. On the other hand, letting it all out helps you a lot; this would reduce the pressure of all your feelings.

5. Stick To Your Routine

When going through a hard time, we stop following our daily routine, sure it is okay to take some time off from work, but it is not okay to stop eating. When going through a heartbreak, many people stop eating correctly, start sleeping more in the mornings, and just kind of mess their routine. But now is the time to work on yourself, don't stop eating healthy, don't mess up your sleeping habits, and above all, start going to the gym; you can let all the anger and frustration out through some exercise.

6. It Is Time To Make Yourself Feel Special

After a breakup, your sense of self-worth is reduced, a lot of insecurities attack you, but this is not the time to hate yourself; it is the time to love yourself. Don't just sit at home, watching a movie and crying about your breakup; what you can do is get a change. You can go shopping, buy new clothes, jewelry, etc. Get a new haircut, and love the new you. Focus on yourself, become selfish for a while. Now you don't have to think about anyone else, set new goals, and above all, take care of yourself.

Conclusion

Breakups have become very common, so familiar that people sometimes forget what it feels like, but don't worry, and you were not born with this person, try to work on yourself and give yourself the love you deserve. Remember that you are worth someone who cares about you and loves you the way you want to be loved. It is okay to be single; it is the time to try new things and redefine yourself.

Chapter 8:
6 Dating Red Flags To Avoid

When dating someone, there always stands a risk. A risk of not being happy or a threat of choosing the wrong person. That is why elders taught us to make smart decisions smartly. But what can one do when it comes to finding the one. Acknowledging a person you want to date won't be enough. Many factors revolve around dating. That is why it is essential to recognize red flags in your relationship. So, we should never hurry to commit to someone. Take your time. There is a lot more than getting to know this person. When initially dating, we always need to make sure to know where our comfort zone lies.

Red flags are the danger signs of a relationship. It can save you a lot of time and positivity. And it's not necessarily true that only the other person is to blame. Sometimes we fail to give them our part of affection, and gradually it becomes a disaster. Even if we overlook the minor toxicity, ignoring the major red flags is not suitable for you. Don't hesitate to give your opinion.

1. Shortfall Of Trust

The one major thing we all need to date someone is trust. Doubt will only make things difficult for you and your partner. Trusting each other is vital in a relationship. And when you date someone, trust grows slowly. And if your growth is based on lies and cheating, then that trust is as thin as thread. You can't force yourself to trust them either. If it doesn't come naturally, count it as a significant red flag because trust is the first thing that comes when dating someone.

2. Change In Personality

In a relationship, we have often seen people change their personalities around different people. If the same is happening to you, then you have to be careful. If they act differently around you, it indicates that they are not themselves in front of you. That is one major red flag in dating that shouldn't be ignored. They try to act the way you would like, instead of the course you are in. And eventually, they will get frustrated. So, it's better to be yourself around everyone. That way, your relationship will be genuine, and you feel a lot happier.

3. Toxicity

An abusive relationship is the worst kind. When someone is not attentive towards you or shouts at you constantly, you become the submissive one.

It would be best if you took a stand for yourself equally. Most of the time, people stay quiet in times like these. But it's to be known that it is a dangerous sign in your dating life. It's a red flag that needs to be taken into notice. You don't have to cope with them; leave them be. Find someone who matches your energy. A toxic person is just as bad as drugs. We need to be careful around them.

4. Feeling Insecure

Sometimes, a relationship that is not meant to be, leaves you feeling insecure about yourself. You constantly question your place in that relationship. Where do you stand in their life? It leaves you thinking about all the flaws you have and examining all the wrong decisions. You have to know that it works both ways. And whoever they are, they have to accept you no matter what. You start to contribute more than your partner when it should be all about equality.

5. Not Being Around Each Other

When we dive into a relationship, we feel the need to be comforted. And when the person opposite you makes you feel uncomfortable, it's a major red flag in your dating life. You both need to make sure to be there for support. If not, then that relationship doesn't hold any significant meaning. If we do not feel secure or satisfied, then what do we get from this relationship? Because that is the most important thing that we might need from someone. But it's essential to play your part as well. Both sides should give their all for their dating to work.

6. Keeps Secrect From You

What someone needs in a relationship is to share their lives. Talking is the basis of communication that builds a relationship. But if your partner keeps secrets, then how can you grow together? You always need to speak for better understanding and comfort with each other. If they are acting fishy, you can't spy on them. It's a red flag that you need to catch.

Conclusion

You need someone who provides you with what you deserve. If you feel someone is not suitable for you, then feel free to break up with them. It would help if you were your priority. And make sure others know how important you are to yourself and should be important to them too.

Chapter 9:
6 Tips To Have A Healthy Long-Distance Relationship

Who says long-distance relationships don't last? Well, a lot of your friends and family members would be against it, they would discourage it, and will advise you not to take it too seriously as for them, it'll only lead to your heartbreak. Honestly, it's not going to be easy. Long-distance would make most of the things unachievable, it could get complicated at times, and you will find yourself vulnerable, sad, and lonely. However, that extra distance also plays a role in getting both of you closer. Studies have found that long-distance relationships don't differ significantly from geographically close relationships, and even in some cases, it might even be better.

First of all, you should be comforted in knowing that long-distance relationships can succeed. With that in mind, we have combined a list of tips that will keep your long-distance relationship healthy and ensure that it lasts.

Technology Is Your Best Friend

In this age of facetime-ing and texting without paying sky-high rates, long-distance relationships are now easier than ever. You can share the day-to-day minutia with your partner by instantaneously sharing photos, exchanging texts and calls, and skyping one another. It'sIt's much different than writing a letter to your loved one and waiting weeks or months for a response. People in long-distance relationships also rely more heavily on technology to stay connected with each other. This helps them communicate verbally even more than the couples who see each other often, sit in the same room, and do not interact at all. It's essential not just to generalize but to share details with your partner. It would make both of you feel like you've witnessed each other's day.

Be Commited to The Relationship

This implies to everyone involved in relationships, but especially to people who are pursuing long-distance relationships. It's crucial to know that you're committed to only one person and that you love them before wasting your time as well as theirs. If you're choosing to stay in a long-distance relationship, you both must sort out where you both stand in life, what will happen next in your relationship, and that you both work towards a goal. It can be daunting to plan your future around another person, but it can do wonders for you both if we both work it through. Be vocal about your feelings so that the other person doesn't live in darkness about what you want.

Set An End Date

While long-distance love can be magical, but it's only a great thing for a finite time. Eventually, you would crave wanting to be in the same place as your partner. It can be hard to stay apart for a long time. One thing that'll help couples in this drastic time is to schedule a meeting and look forward to it every day. Both must stay equally committed to the relationship and should be on the same page about how long this situation would last. You and your partner's plans should align in eventually living in the same place.

Do Stuff Together, Even Though You're Apart

If you aren't physically in the same place, it doesn't mean you both can't have fun together. You can plan a movie night via skype or cook something together while facetime-ing each other. There are loads of streaming services available that make it easier to binge-watch your favorite shows with your partner. Apart from that, you can also search for some quizzes or games online that will connect both of you and help you find more about each other. You can also raise controversial topics and spark new and exciting conversations to see your partner's stance.

Make Fun Plans For When You Both Will Meet

Indulge into details of what the two of you will do the next time you see each other. Make it a ritual of discussing all of the stuff with your partner that you so eagerly look forward to doing with them. Be it trying new restaurants every day, or picking up a holiday destination, or simply choosing a new hobby to do together. You can also schedule good night video calls in your PJs to create a sense of you going to bed together.

Set Clear Rules and Boundaries

Don'tDon't do anything that you wouldn't expect your partner to do either. Try your best to stay out of situations that might make your partner feel insecure or uncomfortable. You don't have to check in with your partner for every approval, but you should set clear boundaries for the both of you and adhere to them.

Conclusion

It can get lonely and difficult sometimes when dealing with long-distance but know that the fruits, in the end, will be as sweet as heaven. Constantly inject positive energy into your relationship to keep it alive. Be grateful for your partner and be thankful for the fact that there's someone who loves you and whom you love.

PART 2

Chapter 1:
10 Signs You're Falling In Love

As our Literature master, Shakespeare, once said, 'A heart to love, and in that heart, courage, to make's love known.'

Ah, love! A four-lettered small word that leaves such a heavy impact on people. Falling in love is nothing short of a beautiful experience, but it can also give you a veritable roller-coaster of emotions. From feeling unsure to terrifying, disgusting, exhilarating, and excited, you might feel it all. If your mobile screen pops up and you're hoping to see their name on the screen, or you're looking for their face in a crowd full of thousands, then you, my child, are doomed! You are well familiar with the feeling of getting butterflies just by hearing their voice, the urge to change your wardrobe completely to impress them, the constant need to be with them all the time. It is known that people who are in love tend to care about the other person's needs as they do their own.

You often go out of their way for their happiness. Whether it's something as small as making their favorite dish or impressing them with some grand gestures, you always try to make them feel content and happy.
If you're in the middle of some casual inquiry into whether you're falling in love, then we are here to help you. Below are some signs for you to discover if it's really just simply a loss of appetite or if you're merely lovesick.

1. **You don't hesitate to try new things with them:**

One of the factors that you could look into is that you become fearless and more adventurous when you are in love. You don't hang back to step out of your comfort zone and engage in all your partner favors' activities and interests. Suddenly the idea of trying sushi or wearing something bright doesn't seem so crazy. You are willing to be more daring and open to new experiences. You are ready to go on that spontaneous trip with them and make memories, all while being a little scared inside. But isn't love all about trying new things with your partner? The New York Times article in 2008 revealed that people in a relationship who try new hobbies together help keep the spark alive long after the honeymoon phase is over.

2. **You're always thinking about them:**

When you are in love, you always tend to think about your partner. Rehash your last conversation with them, or simply smiling at something they said, or questions like what they must be doing right now, have they eaten their meal yet, did they go to work on time or were late again, are always on the back of your mind. You are mentally, emotionally, and physically impacted about caring for them. But it isn't overwhelming. Instead, you get a sense of a calm and secure reality that you will constantly crave. When in love, we tend to merge with that person in such a way that they start to dominate our thoughts and we become wholly preoccupied with them.

3. **You become anxious and stressed:**

According to a psychology study, falling in love could also cause higher levels of cortisol, a stress home, in your body. So the next time you feel jittery or anxious, that person might mean more to you than you think. You might become anxious to dress up nicely to impress them, or if they ask you something, the pressure of answering them intellectually can be expected. But suppose you're feeling overly anxious about your partner, like them not texting you back instantly or thinking they might be cheating on you. In that case, it's an indication of insecure attachment, and you might want to work on yourself to avoid feeling like this.

4. **You become inspired and motivated:**

A few days ago, you needed the motivation to get out of bed. And now, the future suddenly seems so bright and full of potential. Your partner inspires you to set up new goals, have a positive attitude, and cheer you from behind while you feel full of energy and chase them. When we are in love, a part of our brain, considered the reward system, releases excess dopamine, and we feel invincible, omnipotent, and daring. Your life becomes significantly better when you're around them.

5. **You become empathetic towards them:**

It's not a secret that you start seeing your partner as an extension of yourself and reciprocate whatever they feel when you fall in love. Suppose they are accepted into their favorite program, or they expect to receive that interview call, or their favorite football team might have lost in the quarters. In that case, you might feel the same excitement, happiness, or distress that your partner does. Becoming empathetic towards your partner means making sacrifices for them, like going to the grocery store because your partner is tired or refueling their tank in the cold so that they don't have to step out. According to an expert, "Your love is growing when you have an increased sense of empathy toward your partner. When they feel sad, you feel sad. When they feel happy, you feel happy. This might mean going out of the way to give them love in the way that they want to receive it, even if it is not the way you would want to receive love."

6. It's just plain easy:

You don't have to put in extra effort, and it doesn't seem to drain your energy. Instead, you feel energized and easy. You can be your complete, authentic self around them. And it always just seems to go with the flow. Even the arguments don't feel much heated as they did in the other relationships. When you're in love, you prioritize your partner over your pride and ego. You don't hesitate to apologize to them and keep your relationship above everything. When you are with your partner, and it doesn't feel like hard work, know that they are the one!

7. You crave their presence:

Some theorists say that we are more drawn to kissing, hugging, and physical touch when we fall in love. Physical closeness releases a burst of the love hormone termed Oxytocin, which helps us feel bonded. Of course, you don't want to come as someone too clingy who is permanently attached to his partner's hip, but knowing where your person is or how their day went is what you should be looking forward to. On the flipside, Corticotrophin is released as part of a stress response when we are away from our partner, which can contribute to anxiety and depression.

8. You feel safe around them:

It takes a lot of courage for people to open up to their partners. If you don't mind being vulnerable around them, or if you've opened up to them about your dark past or addressed your insecurities, and they have listened contently to you and reassured you. You have done vice versa with your partner, then that's just one of the many signs that you both are in love with each other. Long-lasting love gives you a solid ground and a safe space where you can be upset and vulnerable. When we feel an attachment to our partner, our brain releases the hormones vasopressin and Oxytocin, making us feel secure.

9. You want to introduce them to your family and friends:

You just never shut up about your love interest over the family dinner or when hanging out with your friends. They know all about them, from their favorite spot in the city to the color of their eyes, to how much you adore them and want to spend every single minute talking about them. And now all your family members and friends are curious to meet the guy/girl they have been listening about for the past few weeks. You want to introduce them into every aspect of your life and want it to last this time. So, you make perfect arrangements for them to meet your friends and family, and on the other hand, threatens them to behave Infront of him/her.

10. You care about their happiness:

When you put them and their feelings first, that's how you know it's true love. You don't just want happiness for yourself only, but instead wants it in excess measure for your partner. According to marriage researchers at UC Berkeley, " Spouses who love each other stay together longer, be happier, and support each other more effectively than couples who do not love each other compassionately." You want to go out of your way, or do their favorite thing, to see a smile on their face.

Conclusion:

If you relate to the signs above, then you've already been hit by the love cupid. Scientists have discovered that falling in love, is in fact, a real thing. The brain releases Phenylethylamine, a hormone known for creating feelings of infatuation towards your significant other. The mix and match of different hormones released in our body while we are in love are wondrous. If you have gotten lucky and found a special someone for yourself, then cling to them and don't let them go! If you found this video helpful, please like and subscribe to the channel. Also don't forget to share this video with someone who you find might benefit from this topic as well!

Chapter 2:
How To Survive a Long Distance Relationship

Today we're going to talk about a very touchy yet important subject. If you have a partner who's not local, or you know that they are going to move countries some day, you've gotta be prepared for that time to come. You've got to be sure whether you will begin a long distance relationship or whether you will move to that country to be with that person.

For the purpose of this video, I am going to assume that you have already committed to being in a long distance relationship. And as with any commitment, you have got to be willing to make compromises and sacrifices to maintain that relationship.

There are a couple of things that you will have to mentally prepare yourself for if you are in it for the long haul with this person. They could be gone for days, weeks, months, or even years. First of all you have to ask yourself, are you okay with seeing this person only once every few months? Will you be happy if you wont be able to spend majority of the time with the person throughout the year? How will you cope with the distance? Are you okay with not having physical intimacy with the person? Will you be willing to sacrifice your freedom to wait for this person to return? And can you trust this person to be faithful to you as you spend all your time apart?

For me personally, I was committed to a Long distance relationship once before. And it was the hardest thing for me to do. Especially when it came time at the airport for the send off.

Having already known prior that it would happen someday, i still went ahead with the relationship. All was well and all was fun, but time soon caught up with us and before i knew it, it was already time to say goodbye... temporarily at least. I must admit that it was tough... It was tough because we have gotten so used to spending time together physically in the same space for so long, that this sudden transition was all foreign territory to me. Not being able to touch each other, not being able to meet up for meals, not being able to just hang out at the movies, and not to mention the time zone difference. These were all very real challenges. And they were incredible hard especially in the first few months. I cried at the airport, i cried on the drive home, I was incredibly unhappy, and i was not prepared in any capacity whatsoever to feel this way. You never really know how to feel about something until it actually happens to you.

Knowing that the next time we would see each other would be months away, there was no way to know how to feel or act when suddenly it feels like a limb has been chopped off and you are just struggling to find your feet again. I looked to friends for social support and that was the thing that got me through the toughest periods. Sure we could still FaceTime and call and whatever. Especially in this day and age, but it was still tough having a relationship over the computer. It does feel like on some level you're dating virtually. Everything had to change and I had to relearn what it meant to be in a relationship all over again. I wasn't ever a sappy or clingy boyfriend. I know that about myself. But I do have an expectation to meet up maybe once or twice in a week. Now it's once or twice a year. And it's not fun at all.

So now I put that question back to you, after hearing this part of the story, are you willing to put yourself through this? Or would it be easier if you just chose someone who is in the same physical space with you with no plans on leaving town. If you were to ask me, I might actually do it all over again with someone like that.

The next thing that you've got to have to survive a long distance relationship, is to have a strong social support group. A group of friends that you can share your troubles with. People who can empathise with you, and people who can spend time with you in lieu of your partner. You never want to be in a situation where your partner is your entire world, because when they leave, you will most likely crumble. If you relied on them for all your happiness, their sudden absence will certainly leave you devastated. If u do not have a strong support network of friends, i would suggest you think doubly hard about committing to a long distance relationship.

Now comes the most important part, in my opinion, of having a successful long distance relationship. And that is trust. Trust in each other to be faithful, and trust in each other to do the right thing at all times.

I will bring back to my experience with my long distance relationship. To keep things short, after about a year into my LDR, i discovered that my partner had been cheating on me many times over. And my whole world did come crashing down. Having thought that everything was going according to plan up until that point, i was completely blindsided by the avalanche that hit me. It really hit me hard. But I knew that i loved myself more, and so I packed my bags and flew back home from the trip.

Getting over the relationship was relatively easy because i knew there was nothing left there anymore. There was no more trust to come home to. I had no faith in the relationship anymore and it was effectively over for me. It may sound too easy watching this video, but trust me i went through a great deal and I was incredibly happy with my decision. I learned that i was incredibly resilient and that even though things didn't work out the way i had hoped, and even though my vision of the future was changed drastically, it didn't knock me down. And I chose myself first.

So my question that I put to you now is, to what extent do you trust your partner to be faithful to you? Has he or she cheated on you before? Have they always chosen you first? Can you touch your heart and say they will never do anything to hurt you? Or are you too naive like I was to believe that all is well? Because I was incredibly confident at one point that we were making the LDR work beautifully. Until it suddenly didn't. Would you be okay if you found out that your partner was cheating on you secretly overseas while you guys were apart? Would you be paranoid of the things he could do? If you can answer these things honestly, then u might be able to LDR make it work for you. If not, again, do reconsider your relationship now.

For me personally, If you don't know my stance by now, I absolutely do not believe in LDR. Especially if it's a permanent period. If your partner is gone maybe for a 3-6 month work trip. Yeah maybe that's doable, but if they are gone for 5-6 years and if there's a big question mark behind that... I would totally back away. It would be a deal breaker for me.

The thing with relationships is that, I believe it is the physical presence, the physical connection, the physical communication, and the physical touch that keeps two people together. Without any of these things on a regular basis, it is likely that a couple with drift apart on some level... And without these things, one might be tempted to seek comfort and physical intimacy elsewhere if they can't wait another 5 months before they can see you again.

But if your foundation is incredibly strong, if you guys have made a commitment, if you guys trust each other completely, and if you believe that your relationship can weather any storm, then I already think that you know you can handle a long distance relationship. I am simply here to affirm to you what you already know.

But take me as a word of warning that even strong relationships do fail in the face of a long distance relationship. So you have to be prepared to handle anything that comes your way.

I hope I have been able to shed some light into this topic for you.

Take care and I'll see you in the next one.

Chapter 3:
What To Do When Your Partner Cheats On You

We all know someone who has been cheated on or someone who did the cheating, or maybe there is a chance that someone cheated on you. When something like this happens, everyone involved in this gets disturbed. When you find out that your significant other cheated on you, you feel betrayed, and the first emotion you show is anger, and you just want to leave; fight or flight is a natural response. A therapist says that you should never make an instant decision because once you calm down, you will see that there is a lot to lose, and you might also have children to consider. However, you will be conflicted as to what you should do. Here are some of the things you should do once you find out your partner is cheating.

1. Assess Your Partner's Attitude Regarding Cheating

Some people cheat as a one-time thing, and some have entire relationships on their hiding side. Whether it is an isolated thing or something that happens regularly, you should have a heart-to-heart with your partner whenever you find about it. When you are doing that, you should pay attention to their attitude, notice if your partner is in denial, make excuses, or blame you. If they do that, this means they are not ready to change. Still, if your partner is ashamed and recognizes they have a problem and are ready to change that, that is a good sign.

2. Speak to a Couple's Therapist

However, as much as you may speak to your therapist about your cheating partner, going to one with your partner can likewise help decide whether both of you can find ways to work things out. Also, you may think about how you'll at any point have the option to trust your better half once more, and an objective party could help you sort it out. "Conceding and remedying awful conduct, revamping trust, and pardoning are the principal issues you need to confront," Most of the time, affairs occur because the communication and intimacy in the relationship have broken down. Both parties must approach the problem with a sincere wish to discover what went wrong and fix it. Forgiveness is an important part of the healing process, whether the couple stays together or not. A therapist said, "While I don't think you should stay together and suffer if nothing's working, in my practice, I see many couples who do the work and wind up happier than before."

3. Ask Yourself If You Can Forgive Them

It is not easy to forgive someone who has cheated on you, but if you want to continue your relationship with them, that is the necessary part. Forgiving, of course, does not mean that you condone what happened or that it would be fine if it happens again but actually, what it means is that you want to close this chapter and move on. It is essential to create mutual forgiveness. Else, you will be stuck in blaming each other and defending yourself, and you will never be able to move forward from there.

4. Figure Out If You Still Love Each Other

Sometimes, love trumps everything, but other times, it's not enough. "Do you still love each other, and is it mutual? "Love is a lot more like a partnership than romance. Loving each other means focusing on what you want from your partner and being concerned with their happiness, too. Discussing <u>how you give and receive love</u> will improve your relationship and help you understand what makes each of you feel loved and express love effectively. The foundation of lasting love is the ability to work through things together."

Chapter 4:
6 Relationship Goals To Have

We live in a generation where the term "relationship goals" has become a part of the trendy vernacular. It may seem more like a hashtag than anything else, but we all are eager to go into the depth of its meaning. A beautiful photo of a stunning couple having a good time together? Relationship goals. A cute text message sent to a girlfriend from his boyfriend? Relationship goals. A perfect wedding? Relationship goals. All these might seem sweet and enviable and look like an absolute dream, and it doesn't mean that these come off as accessible to them. If you have ever been in a relationship, you would know exactly what I'm saying.

Love is not always fireworks, passion, and butterflies. Relationships are not just date nights, kisses, and cuddles. And love is not that glamorous as it looks on social media. But when you strive to build something together, involving your selflessness, commitment, and even sweat and tears, those are actual relationship goals. Here is a list of what relationship goals you must have with your partner.

1. **Always Do New Things Together**

Sure, alone time might be great, but together time is where the magic happens too. Avoiding your relationship becoming mundane and a rut, you both should try to do new things together. This could be choosing any vacation spot or having an exciting adventure together. You both should make a list of all the things you want to do with each other and keep adding stuff that might pop later. Tick things off as you go, and you'll never run out of things to do together.

2. Be Each Other's Biggest Supporters

Perhaps one of the best things about being in a relationship is that you'll always have someone in your corner. Regardless of how crazy or unrealistic your dreams and goals may sound, your partner should be your biggest supporter. Seeing the person you love believing in could come off as a massive motivation to achieve your goals. This goes both ways; both men and women need to feel emotionally supported. You both should take some time out to discuss what emotional support looks like to you, what and when you need it, and then provide the said support for each other.

3. Put Each Other First

Putting each other first in your relationship will ensure that you're paying attention to each other's needs and making sure they are being met. You have become selfless with each other, and you both strive to make each other happy and would do anything to put a smile on each other's faces. You complement each other, protect each other, support and love each other, no matter the obstacles or circumstances.

4. Know The Importance of Alone Time

As much as you don't want to keep your hands off your partner in the early stages of your relationship, it's essential to know that you both need time alone to recharge and refill your cup. Spending all of your time together isn't sustainable, and alone time is significant. It will help you maintain your individuality, allow you breathing space, and encourage a closer relationship with each other when you spend time together.

5. Keep The Physical Connection Going

Sex isn't always an option when dealing with different phases of your relationship. There are going to be times when it might not be physically or mentally possible. But this in no way means that you should stop all physical connections. Physically touching the person you love releases an oxytocin hormone; this feel-good love hormone reduces stress and makes you feel wonderful things. You can stay physically connected by holding hands, cuddling, or simply leaning on one another.

6. Speak Positively About Each Other

Speaking ill of your partner with others is not only disrespectful to them, but it's also disrespectful to your relationship. Sure, you can vent in tough times, but make sure you talk about the actions and behaviors that upset you and not their personality traits. Always speak positively and kindly of each other. Even if their behavior irritates you, focus more on the characteristics you love of them and let it pass.

Conclusion

Relationships are complicated but beautiful at the same time. As simple as the above factors may sound to you, these things take a lot of effort and hard work to be implemented. But when you do all of these with the person you love the most in the world, then all of it can be worth it.

Chapter 5:
What Happens When You Get Bored In A Relationship

Being bored in your relationship can make you feel unpleasant emotions; you would not feel like yourself. You will be more likely to be over things that excited you before, like sex, date night, vacation with your partner, etc. Even if you don't feel like ending things, the lack of satisfaction would be enough to get you frustrated and ready to break up. Due to this boredom, you may feel stuck in a tedious cycle or feel suffocated. There are many things you will notice about yourself when you are bored of your relationship.

Picking unnecessary fights with your partner is one of the signs that you are bored with them. Dr. Binita Amin, a clinical psychologist, says getting into arguments for innocuous reasons might signify you are bored. If you find yourself bickering with your partner for petty reasons, then you may want to step back and assess why. Boredom can efficiently fuel arguments, but disagreements happen in any relationship; the best way is to see if these arguments are indeed caused by boredom.

Your frustration with your relationship causes these arguments. You can always figure out what is exactly causing this boredom, and maybe you can overcome this problem and carry out a healthy relationship.

Sometimes, we all enjoy comfortable silence, but is that silence comfortable anymore, or is it just because you have no more to speak to each other. Silent meals even when you are in a sit-in restaurant, or even if a few words are exchanged, but those words are in safe and predictable confines, then that is a sign that you are bored. To prevent this, you can try strengthening your bond with your partner.

When we first meet a person we like or at the beginning of a relationship, we put our best self forward, we try to be perfect for them, but when a person feels bored, they no longer place any effort into their relationship. They don't bother looking nice for a date night or don't bother waiting for them at the dinner table because we all know such factors lead to a healthy relationship. Being bored in a relationship can lead to an unhealthy period of your life. But if you are putting in the effort, you know that boredom is far away from your relationship and you.

Have you ever wondered about what it would be like to be with someone else? Even when you are in a relationship. If you have, then that is a sign that you have fallen victim to boredom. It is natural for a person to find more than one person attractive but always pay attention to what is the factor that is causing you to daydream about someone else, and it is simply because you are bored with your relationship. Because if that is the case, you need to make your relationship more exciting or talk and discuss matters with your partner.

Many people in this world are happy to be single, as they say, to be free of any commitment but are that the case with you. Do you wish that you were single? Or envying the single status of your friends? If yes, then you need to take a closer look at your relationship; it may turn out that you feel bored with your relationship, that you no longer feel the passion and excitement of the earlier days of your relationship. If you are glad that your partner is busy with something else, then that is a sign that you are bored.

Don't let boredom be the end of your relationship; you can seek help from relationship counselors, or you can sit around and discuss these matters. Together you can always find a solution to every problem. All relationship requires efforts, so put in your step and let your relationship bloom.

Chapter 6:
Feeling Insecure In Your Relationship

No matter how perfect a relationship sounds or seems, there is always something that pushes you off on the opposing side. That is feeling insecure. This feeling of being insecure is what makes us doubt ourselves and our partners. A relationship needs to build around trust and feeling secure in it. When you lack those factors, it's only natural that you might fall now or then; it often happens when you feel like your needs are not getting fulfilled by your partner. You will eventually come to realize that you wanted something else. It also occurs when you keep all the problems to yourself, thus, not trusting each other enough to share. These problems then become your demise, and eventually, you are unable to take them. You realize that going separate ways is the only option when you need a good conversation about your problems and listening to what your partner has to say. Giving them a chance and solving your problems together is how you will strengthen your bond, and that's how you will overcome your fears, as we all know that trust is the foundation of any relationship.

It would be best if you let go of things. When you start a relationship with a person you care about, you learn to leave something behind. You watch movies that they like or eat the food they want. Sacrifice is a common ground you both walk on. You have to learn to go by their choices sometimes. But, the same should be done with you. They should do the same for you, if not more. You both need to make some compensations along the way of your relationship. You have to give each other choices. You have to trust each other enough to know that they might be doing the right thing for you or making the right choice for you.

So, the most common factor is trust. Many relationships have been broken because of a lack of confidence. Trust comes very handily when you need to go through a difficult phase of your life. You need the support of your partner, and you just need them by your side. That means trusting them to stay with you through your worst. Growing together is what you need to fulfill in a relationship. And sometimes, while doing so, we meet disappointment. Lack of trust drives you to get annoyed quickly, and you start to get distant. Growing apart may seem complicated, but you think it's better than stay together. These insecurities are very hard to overcome, and all you would need is time. But, know that it is your mind speaking most of the time. That is why taking a chance is such a considerable risk that we sometimes do not bother with it. We have to game risk to know if there is a spark between you two to keep all the light alive. Or if it is just a dead end.

It would be best if you gave yourself a lecture on positivity now and then. It would help if you got rid of all the evil thoughts that are driving you towards doubt. Gain more confidence in yourself and gain more confidence in your partner. Believe in each other. Try to stay positive in every situation. And believe in the best possible outcome of your situation in your relationship. Surround yourself with good thoughts and feelings. Always motivate your partner in the best way possible and think of them as your equal. Share everything, good or bad, with them. You will see getting rid of your insecurities slowly by taking these small measures towards your relationship.

You just need to overcome your differences by talking and listening. Both of you need a little break now and then. You need to give them space often, but not such that they start to believe you are ignoring them. You need to shower your attention and make sure that this whole relationship works out in your favor. Don't get jealous of their interaction with another gender, but trust them to be loyal to you. Give them love and receive love from them. Insecurities are often built on false rumors or accusations. It would help if you stopped a little to process every time. And just know that in this case, your partner's words matter greatly. Make it work out, and try to feel as secure as possible with them around you.

Chapter 7:
7 Signs You Have Found A Keeper

Are you looking for Mr. or Mrs. Right? Or do you think you have found the right person, but how can you be sure? Sometimes, we meet someone who seems like the person you would want to spend your whole life with, but during those times, someone is in for a quick hookup. The only partners worth keeping are the ones that give you the positive vibes that you need after a dull and tedious day, the ones that make you feel happy, and your relationship doesn't feel boring at all. Here are signs that you have found a keeper.

1. **They inspire you to become a better person:**

When we meet someone very kind, helpful and overall a friendly person that person usually inspires us to be better and luckily the world is full of friendly people. Is your partner like this too? Is he warm, kind, and helpful? Does he inspire you to become a better version of yourself? Then you know you have found yourself a keeper. You know you have found the right person when your partner works hard, gives you and his family time, and has his life organized.

2. They are always there:

There are times when we all suffer when things get tough to handle. At times like these, a person always needs support and love to get through the hard times. If your partner is there for you even when you can't defend yourself and they cheer you up, you know that this is a keeper. A perfect partner is someone who knows how to make you laugh even when you are crying, your partner will never believe the things people talk about behind your back, and he would never hesitate to lend you a hand when you need some help.

3. They know you more than yourself:

Sometimes it fascinates us how someone can know us more than we know ourselves; it feels perfect when someone knows how or what we are thinking. If your partner knows what you are feeling without telling them, then they are the one. Does your partner know what you are comfortable with? Can they tell when you feel upset? Do they motivate you to do better and ask you to chase after your dreams? If so, then don't waste more time thinking if this is the right person for you because it is.

4. Your interests are common:

Sure, opposites attract, but too many differences are not usually suitable for someone's relationship. It would help if you had a common interest with your partner, like having common beliefs, values, and religious perspectives. When you agree on these things, your bond will become more robust, and you would find it very easy to live with that person.

5. They are honest with you:

Finding an honest person is a tiring thing to do; many people lie more than twice a day, but how can that affect your relationship? The right one may lie about small things that don't matter that much, like whether the color suits you or not; they may say those things to make you feel good about yourself, but lying about other things like financial status, health, or fidelity can be more serious. A true keeper would never keep these things from you, and they would always be honest with you even if the truth upsets you.

6. They don't feel tired of you:

Although everyone needs some space, even from the person they love the most, he will never get tired of you if he is the one. Your partner will never feel bored with you; on the contrary, your partner will never get tired of looking at you, admiring you, being with you, and above all, love you. When a person is so in love with you that they want to spend every second of their life with you, then you know you have found a keeper.

7. You are a part of their dreams:

Can your partner not even imagine your life without you? Has your partner already planned his future, and you are a big part of it? If so, you know that this one's a keeper. You both have reached a point in your lives where even thinking about living without each other sounds absurd, and then you know that you have found a keeper.

Conclusion:

A keeper is someone that loves, cherishes, and cares for you like no one has ever had. Don't worry if you haven't found your keeper, and it is just a matter of time before you do because, for every one of us, there is someone out there.

Chapter 8:
6 Behaviours That Keep You Single

Dating may not be as easy as it is shown in all those romantic Hollywood movies. There is so much more than appearance and stability in dating someone. And when you are old enough to be involved with someone, you sometimes find yourself uninterested. You think about how everyone your age has already started dating while you are back there eating junk and watching Netflix. It might appear to you that being in a relationship is tiresome, and you stop trying for it. Everyone has a different preference when it comes to finding someone for themselves. You tend to look for someone that matches your knight in the shining armor, which makes it hard for you to find someone you need.

Be true to you yourself while finding someone to date. Looking for someone with the expectation that you are rich and handsome would be foolish. It would be best if you worked on yourself more than that. Make yourself ease around with people but no so much that they start to get annoyed. Don't get in your way.

1. **Trust Is Essential**

Trusting each other is an important factor for dating someone. If you don't trust your partner even in the slightest, then nothing will matter. You will constantly doubt each other. Both of you will eventually fall apart if there is no trust. And if you have trust issues, it will be difficult for you to find someone worthy. But, if you trust too quickly, then it's only natural that you will break your bubble of expectations. Be friendly. Try to get to know them properly before making any assumptions about them. You don't want to go around hesitating about everything. Find yourself a reliable partner that trusts you too.

2. **Too Many Expectations**

Expecting too much from your partner will lead to only one thing. It leads towards Disappointment. It would help if you let them be. Don't expect things to go your way always. Your knight in the shining armor may be a bookworm because people find love in the most unexpected places. It doesn't always mean to keep no expectations at all. To keep the expectations low. You will get surprised constantly when you don't know what's coming your way. Don't let people cloud your judgment, and keep high standards about a relationship. Everyone has their share of ups and downs. Comparison with others will not be suitable for your relationship.

3. **Have Self-Confidence**

One has to respect itself before anything else can. You have to have self-esteem in you for people to take you seriously. It is true "you can't love someone unless you learn to love yourself first." You tend to feel insecure about yourself. Everything around you seems too perfect for you. And you constantly think that your partner will stop loving you one day. That fear of yours will get you nowhere. Try to give yourself as much care you can. It doesn't hurt to be loved.

4. Don't Overthink

You found a guy, and He seems to be excellent. But you start to overthink it. Eventually, you let go. That is what you shouldn't have done. Just try to go with the flow sometimes. Don't try too hard for it. Go for it the easy way. Overthinking will lead you to make up scenarios that never happened. Just let it be and see where it goes. Be easy so people can approach you. Think, don't overthink.

5. Involving Too Many People

When you initially start dating, you get nervous. People get help from their friends sometimes. But it is not necessary to get every move through them. Involving them in everything will only get your partner get uncomfortable and get you frustrated. People tend to give a lot of opinions of their own. You will get confused. So, it is good to keep these things to yourself. Be mindful in giving them a brief report from time to time. However, keep them at a reasonable distance.

6. Giving Up Too Quickly

If it doesn't work initially, it does not mean that it will never work. Patience is an essential element when it comes to dating anyone. Don't give up too quickly. Try to make it work until it's clear that it won't. Give it your all. Compromise on things you can. Because if both of you are not willing to compromise, it will not work between you both. It will work out in the end if it's meant to be. Don't push it if it's not working too.

Conclusion

It is hard; it keeps going at a pace. But all you must need is that spark that keeps it alive. Make it work until it doesn't. Go for it all. Make commitments only when you are sure about your choice. And be true to your words. Who wants to be single forever?

Chapter 9:
9 Signs of a Toxic Relationship

Before getting into the video, let's talk about what's a toxic relationship? Dr. Lillian Glass, a California-based psychology expert defines the toxic relationship as "any relationship [between two people who] don't support each other, where there's conflict and one seeks to undermine the other, where there's competition, where there's disrespect and a lack of cohesiveness."

Signs of toxic relationships are all around us. The question is how do we know if we have one? And what are the exact signs of such a relationship? In this video, I'm going to tell you 9 main signs of a toxic relationship. So let's get right into it.

Main

1. Unhealthy Communication Patterns

Passive aggressiveness, aggressive or bullying styles of conversations that your partner engages with you could be a clear sign that something isn't right between the two of you. The relationship can turn toxic very quickly when either partner feels guilted into responding in a submissive way to please the other. Furthermore bad communication can also lead to avoiding talking to your partner. Instead of treating you with love and compassion, if your partner has animosity, criticism, sarcasm, and egoism in most of his conversations with you, then it can lead to hatred and thus poison the relationship. We all want a partner who can speak to us with kindness and understanding rather than someone who speaks to us in a threat-like manner.

2. Habits or Cycles of Cheating and lying

If you feel that your partner is cheating on you or lying to you, it will damage your trust in your partner and may also harm the relationship. Once trust is lost, it is very difficult to get it back. You may start to trust your partner in days or months, but the possibility always seems fragile. Relationships with distrust can turn good partners into jealous or suspicious people. Sometimes even your partner's unforgettable compromises can't repair trust if it is badly broken. So, if for some reason you can't trust your partner then the relationship is definitely toxic.

3. Your Loved Ones Strongly Disapproves of Your Partner

What people close to you think of your partner is one of the most important factors in determining whether the relationship is beneficial or one that could be toxic. So, make sure to pay close attention to what your friends, family, and loved ones are saying about your partner.

Your family and friends always want you to be safe and happy, so if they strongly dislike your partner then there must be a strong reason behind it. They may be able to see red flags in them that you might have otherwise overlooked that may point towards something toxic brewing. That reason or some hateful reactions of your loved ones against your partner can indicate that the relationship is not good for you.

4. Over-Dependency On Your Partner

It has been noted by several personality experts that those who are the least self-sufficient (but also most self-critical) tend to be the most toxic partners. Sometimes this is a symptom of an underlying relationship problem. Sometimes it is not. But when a partner is absent-minded or disinterested in "self-care", that can be a red flag.

5. Constant Fears of Being Judged

Signs of toxic relationships can also include the feeling like you are constantly being judged. You may wonder why you always feel like you need to be on your best behavior. Or, you may think that you always get in trouble with your partner. Some partners can even pick fights as a way of getting back at their relationship - and then some feel like nothing's ever going right.

6. Feeling like you are being taken advantage of

One of the most important signs of toxic relationship behavior is feeling like you're being exploited. You may feel like you're not really treated with care or value. Perhaps you question whether or not you are important enough. You may worry that your partner sees you as someone they can take for granted.

In fact, one of the core dynamics of toxic relationships is that the less valuable you feel, the less valuable your partner will feel. When you have a deep, internal belief that you are not significant, it can lead to behaviors that are meant to hurt you.

7. You Are Always Defending Your Partner

One classic sign of toxic relationship behavior is when you find yourself defending your partner against charges of hurting you or you feel guilty and always come first to apologize to your partner but you are not sure why.

When the lines of communication between you and your partner start to break down, you may find yourself defending your partner instead of talking to solve problems. When you and your partner argue, you may also hear your partner say things like "you just need to learn to get along with people," "your problem is with you, not with me" or "you just want to ruin my life." Such behavior is enough to call the relationship toxic.

8. All the compromise comes from you

Nobody can manage a good relationship with a partner if they are the only one doing all compromise, work, and love.

A good relationship can only be built with the cooperation of both life partners. However, if you do everything while your partner does nothing and never gives the relationship a better chance to improve, then, of course, the relationship is toxic to you.

9. Your Partner Suffers From Addictions

The use of drugs, especially alcohol or (maybe) cigarettes, has a devastating effect on all relationships and is a major reason for leaving relationships. If your partner is addicted to drugs, and you think you can't solve the problem then make sure to provide him/her medical help.

But if he/she is not ready at all to get rid of drugs and drinks too much alcohol regularly, you should consider the relationship toxic.

Closing

So that's it. We are done with our today's topic.

Remember that if you feel that you are in a toxic relationship, don't forget to seek help. Consult your friends and family, be open to their opinions and don't be afraid to end the relationship if it indeed turns out to be toxic. Remember that we only have one life to live and we deserve to be with a partner that can care and love us unconditionally in all the right ways.

Now it's your turn to share your thoughts. Do you know about any other signs of a toxic relationship? Let us know in the comments below. If you got value then hit the like and subscribe button.

PART 3

Chapter 1:
7 Reasons Why Men Cheat

Men and women may cheat for different reasons, but it's likely due to the way men and women are socialized rather than any innate differences between them. The more we, as a society, move away from socialization and patriarchy, the less we see those gender differences in cheating behavior. However, nonetheless, research shows that men are more likely to cheat than women. The ratio is 20% of men have admitted to cheating compared to 13% of women.

We should never forget that our minds are more resilient than we give them credit for. Cheating in a relationship is solely that person's fault, no matter the circumstances. It can always be avoided if the person wants to. There are many reasons why men cheat, along with what defines cheating and signs to watch out for. Here are some reasons and behaviors that might apply to people of all genders but could be relevant to men.

1. They're Looking For A Way Out

Sometimes the first step for a man to get out of a relationship is to cheat. Although people of all genders might cheat, for this reason, men are most likely to do it. This is because men are less likely to have difficult conversations with their partners and seldom tell their own needs in a relationship. So, they see cheating as the only way out. Instead of having to bear the difficult conversation with their partner when they're done with their relationship, they escape through it all by the act of cheating and having an affair.

2. They're Looking For A Connection

Cheating doesn't always happen for physical reasons only, despite what gender norms might tell us about men. Feeling unseen, unheard, or disconnected from their partners can also contribute as a factor for it. Men are much less likely to have a sound social support system, and those things can hurt and make them go into a zone where they feel protected. In those instances, if a woman shows compassion and support, they welcome her with open arms. It might start with a friendship with someone who will make him feel better about himself, and hence, an emotional connection forms.

3. They Have Sociopathic or Narcissistic Traits

If a partner has cheated, there could be more than just finding a way out of their relationship. There can be narcissistic tendencies or sociopathic traits involved. They could be someone who doesn't care about their partner's feelings, and they might do it simply because they want to.

When an opportunity to cheat presents itself, they go towards it without giving a damn about their partner.

4. Revenge Cheating

Some people act on their impulses and cheat out of anger, jealousy, or desire revenge. It's not necessary that their partner might have cheated on them; even if they have done something slight to upset them (like having a close friendship with another man), they'll end up cheating on their partner to make a point.

5. Struggles With Substance Abuse

Cheating becomes more likely if one is dealing with a substance abuse problem. Substance addiction can create an impulse-driven and more immature version of ourselves. Many relationships tend to fall apart if one of the two partners has become addicted to a substance and acts subconsciously on their impulse.

6. They Seek Validation

If someone is not getting validation in their relationship, then insecurity and low self-esteem can drive them to cheat. If they don't feel attracted enough to their partner, they may cheat to seek external validation. Sexual issues can also cause someone to look for someone newer to prove themselves to.

7. They're Emotionally Immature

Emotional immaturity is sometimes the core of why men cheat. Since childhood, men are expected and taught not to talk about their feelings and emotions. This inability to speak leads to several issues and conflicts in their relationships. By the time you know it, they are having an affair and cheating on their significant other. Cheating can be an essential consequence of poor judgment, lack of willpower, self-control, and immaturity. A mature man will always talk about his feelings and resolve conflicts and issues with his partner.

Conclusion:

Being cheated on can be the worst trauma anyone can experience, and there can be so many reasons it might have happened in different relationships and contexts. But no matter the reason, it cannot be denied that infidelity forces both of you to step back. Analyze what went wrong and decide how you both want to move forward from there.

Chapter 2:
6 Ways To Flirt With Someone

No matter how confident and bold we assume ourselves to be, we tend to freeze up and utter a wimpy 'hey' when we see our crush approaching us. Flirting doesn't always come easily to everyone, and there's always struggle, awkwardness, and shyness that follows. But, some people are natural-born flirters and just get the dating thing right.

Knowing how to flirt and actually showing someone that you're interested in them sexually or romantically can be a minefield. But once you get your hands on it, you'll probably become an expert in no time. If you struggle with flirting, we've got some tips to help you master the art of flirting and getting your crush's attention. Below are some ways to flirt with someone successfully.

Be Confident But Mysterious

There's nothing sexier than someone who has a lot of confidence. Of course, I'm not talking about being too overconfident, and it will tend to push people away from you. But if you're strutting down the halls as you own them, your crush (and everyone else) will notice you. Don't give away too much of yourself while being confident. People tend to get intrigued by someone who gives off mysterious vibes. They show their interest in you and avail every opportunity to try to get to know you better. This will lead to you having a chance to make up a good conversation with your crush and even flirt with them in between.

Show That You're Interested In Their Life

Who doesn't love compliments and talking about themselves all the time? We come along with people who mostly like to talk than to listen. If you get a chance to talk to your crush, don't waste it. Ask them questions about their life, get to know their views and ideas about certain things like politics, fashion, controversies, show that you're genuinely interested in them. They will love your curious nature and would definitely look forward to having another conversation with you. This will also give your brownie points of getting to know them better.

Greet Them Whenever You Pass Them

Seeing your crush approach you or simply seeing them standing in the halls can be the scariest feeling ever. You will probably follow your gut reaction and become nervous; either you'll walk past them hurriedly or look down at your phone and pretend like you're in the middle of a text conversation battle. But you have to ignore those instincts, and you have to look up at them and simply smile. You don't have to indulge yourself in an extensive conversation with them. Just taking a second to wave or say hi can be more than enough to get yourself on your crush's radar, as you will come off as polite to them.

Make Ever-So-Slight Contact

The sexiest touches are often those electric ones that come unexpectedly, not the intentional ones that might make someone uncomfortable. Unnecessary touches can be a turn-on because they signal a willingness to venture beyond the safe boundaries that we usually maintain between ourselves and others. But be careful not to barge into them accidentally. Small, barely-there touches that only the two of you notice are the best. Let your foot slightly touch theirs or lightly brush past them.

Compliment Them

While everyone loves receiving compliments, try not to go overboard, or they would be more likely to squirm in their seat rather than ask you out. You should compliment them lightly about their outfit or fragrance or their features or personality, but keep the subtle flirtation for when the time and moment is right. Giving them compliments would make them think that you're interested in them and want to step up the equation with them.

Look At Them

Experts suggest that we look and then look away three times to get someone's attention. According to the Social Issues Research Centre, maintaining too much eye contact while flirting is people's most common mistake. Our eyes make a zigzag motion when we meet someone new - we look at them from eye to eye and then the nose. With friends, we look below their eye level to include the nose and mouth. The subtle flirt then widens that triangle to incorporate parts of the body. Please don't stare at someone too intensely, or else you'll end up making them feel uncomfortable.

Conclusion

It might seem nerve-wracking to put yourself out there and start flirting, but fear not! It's normal to get nervous around someone whom you like. Follow the above ways to seem confident and pull off a successful flirtation. Know the importance of keeping a balance between revealing your feelings and keeping the person you like intrigued.

Chapter 3:
6 Ways To Deal With Betrayal

Betrayal is a strong word. And the most challenging part of it is recovery. Healing from something someone has done to you that you were not in favor of can be as hard as counting the number of hair on your head. The first thing that comes in our way is our emotions. Anger, rage, and regret. But, what can one do to save themselves from such a move? They can only be careful with the people around them. Trust issues have always been challenging to deal with. And betrayal only fuels that fire. We often turn to others for support, and sometimes they turn out to be deceivers. It may leave us unprotected.

No doubt that betrayal changes someone to some extinct. The person may feel insecurities within themselves. They start to doubt and stress themselves. It often leads to self-harm, too, at times. And the most severe of them all would be anxiety. Because no matter what, we can't ignore the fact that someone has lied to us and made us believe them. Betrayal is painful. And it's common to have experienced it once in your life. When someone you trusted with your secrets or emotions has broken that trust, that feeling of not being valued enough makes us hate that person, whether they did it intentionally or unintentionally. But there can be some ways to deal with betrayal.

1. Take Time For Emotional Improvement

After a heartbreak, what we need is time. Time to think, time to process, and time to heal. We can't instantly forget about anything that has happened to us. "Time heals all wounds." And that is precisely what we should do. Take a break. Try to do things you want. Make yourself feel light and collected. Stay away from the person who hurt you. This way, it will help you bury that memory quickly. Try to think about it as little as possible. Make sure you have other things on your mind instead. Rearrange your priorities from the start. This time you believe in yourself more than you felt in that person.

2. Overcome Self-Hatred

It is often that you would feel hatred towards yourself. Because you sometimes believe that it was your fault, to begin with. The thing with betrayal is that it is one-sided. The other person can do nothing but suffer. Naturally, you would be pitying yourself for their actions and feeling insecure. But it's not worth your time or emotion. You need to get a hold of yourself and talk some sense into yourself.

3. Try To Forgive and Forget

We all know that it is not as easy as it sounds, but it is more beneficial. When someone betrays us, we feel the need to take revenge. Hurt them the way they hurt us. But nothing can be as comforting as forgetting it ever happened. We all will remember a part of it, but it doesn't have to come between your life. It takes a lot of determination to forgive someone you don't want to ignore, but you will see the pros of it in the future. If you decide you take revenge, then it will leave you guilty and regretful in the future.

4. Ask For Help From The Trusted

It may be difficult for you to trust anyone after being betrayed. But you can always go to someone for comfort. If a possible third party can support you, don't hesitate to reach out to them. Make sure you talk about it with someone so you can take advice and feel light. It will help you to deal with the situation quickly. It will give you the peace of mind that will help you all along the journey ahead. It is recommended to talk with someone who had a betrayal in their life.

5. Acknowledge, Don't React

There is a significant difference between responding and reacting. We should be in control of our emotions. We need to acknowledge our feelings. After betrayal, our senses are more likely to be mixed up, leaving us confused. But that is a recipe for disaster. It will only be harmful to you to react without analyzing the situation appropriately. You can't ignore the fact that you have been hurt, but you will feel calmer by the time.

6. Be Careful Next Time

No one can ensure that we won't get hurt again. But we can be careful around people. That doesn't necessarily mean having trust issues with people but detecting the people who can hurt you. And with each time, you will get better and better at dealing with betrayal. It would help if you felt those emotions to overcome them every single time. And after each series of betrayals, you will become stronger than before.

Conclusion

Betrayal can be heart-wrenching, but it should not stop you from being happy in life. Cry and grieve for a day or two. And then get up again as a stronger person. Believe in yourself. Let go of the past and focus on your future, for it can bring much more happiness.

Chapter 4:
6 Ways To Be More Confident In Bed

Confidence is something a lot of people inherit naturally, while others could work on. When you're confident and comfortable in your skin, people assume that you have a reason to be, and then they react and respect you accordingly. You can be confident all you want at work or on dates, but what about being confident in bed? Being confident sexually can be enjoyable for both you and your partner. It isn't just at ease sexual, but also it's comfortable with the way you express and experience your sexuality.

Sexual confidence can be measured by how authentically you can relate intimately either with yourself or your partner and how pure and vulnerable you are in that sexual space where you feel like giving your 100 percent to be yourself and communicate the pleasure you desire. Building your confidence in bed can crucially improve your sex life. Here are some tips on how to be more confident in bed.

1. Do What You're Already Confident In

Even if you are insecure and think you lack sexual skills, there must be at least a tiny thing that you might be good at. Maybe you don't feel confident enough about your kissing skills, but you're a great cuddler, or perhaps you feel shaky about touching and teasing but are good vocally. Focus on what you're good at and polish that skill every time you're in bed with your partner. This will help you boost your confidence and might even convince you to try something new with them.

2. Try Something New

Once you start considering yourself as the master of that one skill you have been practicing, you would end up craving to try new things. Start with the things you're less comfortable with; maybe stepping out of your comfort zone might be enjoyable for you after all. You neither have to perfect the skill nor be a master of it, just trying it out can be fun in itself. It might be helpful to broaden the sexual script so that it doesn't look the same every time and bore your partner, but instead, trying new things can be an excellent adventure for you as well as your partner.

3. Laugh It Off If You Trip Up

You can't be good at everything you try in bed, nor should you be. What matters is how well you keep your attitude, and if you can have fun with it and have a great laugh if things go south, that's an achievement in itself. If you have already built up consistent self-confidence, then you can laugh it out loud on something that you can't get a grip on. After all, there might always be some things you'll be bad at and others in which you'll be a master.

4. Focus On What You Love About Your Body

There are instances where we will be utterly insecure about our bodies and features. There are some physical traits that we don't like but have made peace with, while others that we want but don't appreciate enough. The next time you look in the mirror, focus more on what you like about your face and body, be confident in them, and the things you don't like about yourself will vanish automatically.

5. Wear What Makes You Feel Confident

There is no particular stuff you have to wear or the way you have to look to feel more confident, but if you wear a look that you think looks great, you must go with it. Chances are, you will start feeling better about yourself instantly. If you feel more confident wearing lipstick, then wear it to bed, or if you think sexier wearing a lotion, use it before bed. Do whatever makes you feel like a total hottie.

6. Repeat A Mantra

We have all heard of the phrase "fake it till you make it." So, there's no harm in faking affirmations till you start believing in them. Keep repeating "I'm confident, I've got this" till it gets through. Affirmations increase how positively we feel about ourselves.

Conclusion

The task of becoming confident may seem daunting, but these small sub-tasks are an easy way to start. Another plus point is once you have practiced these techniques in bed, the confidence will spill over into every area of your life.

Chapter 5:
6 Tips To Find The One

Finding someone who matches our criteria can be a difficult task. We always look for a person who is a knight in shining armor. And by time, we make our type. We are finding someone who looks and behaves like our ideal one. We always fantasize about our right one. No matter how hard it may seem to find someone, we should never lose hope. Sharing is always beneficial. And if you trust someone enough to share your life with them, then it's worth the risk to be taken. The person you chose depends upon you only. The advice can only give you an idea, and you have to act on your own.

Now, when looking for someone from scratch can be difficult for many of us. That person can either be the wrong one or the right one. Only time can tell you that. But you both need to grow together to know if you can survive together. And if not, then separation is the only possible way. But if you find the right one, then it will all be good. You have to have faith in yourself. Be your wingman and go after whatever you desire.

1. Be Patient

When looking for someone you want to spend your time with, someone you want to dedicate a part of your life to, you have to devote your time looking for the one. Be patient with everyone you meet so you will get to know them better. They will be more open towards you when you give them time to open. Doing everything fast will leave you confused. Don't only talk with them. Notice their habits, share secrets and trust them. They will be more comfortable around you when they think that you are willing to cooperate.

2. Keep Your Expectations Neutral

When you find someone for you, they can either leave you disappointed or satisfied. That all depends on your expectations. If you wait for prince charming and get a knight, then you will be nothing but uncomfortable with them. Keep them neutral. Try to make sure that you get to know a person before passing your judgment.

3. Introduce Them To Your Friends

The people who love you tend to get along together. The first thing we do after finding a competitor is telling a friend. We usually go for the people our loved one has chosen for us. While finding the one is all you. They can play a part in giving advice, but they can't decide for you. When we see one, we want everyone to get to know them.

4. Don't Be Discouraged

You are 30 and still haven't found anyone worth your time. If so, then don't get discouraged. That love comes to us when we least expect it. You have to keep looking for that one person who will brighten your days and keep you happy. Please don't go looking for it. It will come to you itself and will make you happy.

5. Look Around You

Sometimes our journey of finding the one can be cut short when we see the one by our side—someone who has been our friend or someone who was with us all along. You will feel happier and more comfortable with finding the right person within your friend. It will make things much more manageable. And one day, you will realize that he was the one all this time. Sometimes we can find one in mutual friends. They may be strangers, but you know a little about them already. However, finding the one within your friend can save you a lot of trouble.

6. Keep The Sparks Fresh

Whatever happens, don't let your spark die because it will become the source of your compassion. It will make a path for you to walk on with your ideal one. Keep that passion, that love alive. If there is no spark, then you will live a life without any light. So, make your partner and yourself feel that compassion in your growth.

Conclusion

Finding one can be a difficult job, but once we find them, they can make us the happiest in the world. And if that person is honest with you, then there is nothing more you should need in one. You can always change your partner until you find the one because they are always their ones too. You have to focus on finding your own.

Chapter 6:
6 Signs You Have Found A Real Friend

Life seems easy when we have someone by our side. Everyone makes at least one friend in their life as if it comes naturally. That one person who we can rely on in difficult times. That one person who cares for us when we forget to care for ourselves. Friends are family that we get to choose ourselves. So, we have to decide that person exceptionally carefully. Friends are people who know who you are. You can share both joy and sadness with them without hesitating.

Friends have a significant impact on our lives. They can change us completely and help us shape ourselves into someone better. However, there might be some forgery in your way. Some people consider themselves as your friend, but we fail to notice that it is otherwise. So, it is imperative to choose a friend carefully, while an essential fraction is dependent on our friendship with someone. A good friend is the one whom you can count on to hold you when you require one. A friend is someone who becomes selfless when it comes to us. They always stay by your side as it said, "friends till the end."

1.You Can Be Yourself Around Them
No matter how you behave in front of your family or co-workers, you can always act like yourself in front of your friend. When they give you a sense of comfort, you automatically become yourself. That is the reason

you never get tired of a friend. Because who gets tired of being who they are. A friend is a person who accepts us with all our flaws and stays by us even in our worst phase. They find beauty in your imperfections. That type of friend becomes necessary to keep around.

2. A Support For Good And Bad Times

We all are aware that support is what we want in our time of need. To share our difficult times and to share our good news with someone. A friend listens. They listen to whatever you want to ramble to them without complaining. They understand you and try to give to advice as well as possible. They are an excellent shoulder to cry on. They feel joy in your happiness. They feel sadness in your loss. Friends are people who love us, and thus, we give them ours in return.

3. You Trust Each Other

Trust is an essential foundation in any friendship. Otherwise, you are meant to fall apart. It would help if you grew that trust slowly. When you are loyal to each other, then there is nothing that comes between you two. You need to develop that trust slowly. When you are dedicated to each other, then there is nothing that comes between you two. Honesty is a must when it comes to building your trust with each other. If even one of you is lying about anything, then that friendship fails. Even if they didn't keep their promise, you can't trust them.

4. They Hype You Up

They won't fall back on complimenting you when you look your best. But a friend won't hesitate to confront you if you don't look good. That is what we like about them, and they won't make you look bad in front of others. They will make sure you know you are worth it. They will make you work for what you deserve. Friends will always try to hype you up and will accolade you. They know what you like and don't, so they shape you like you want to be shaped.

5. You Share Almost Everything

Two friends are always together in spirits. When something noteworthy happens in your life, you always feel the need to share it with someone. That someone will probably be a friend. You tend to share every little detail of any event of your life with them comfortably. They listen to you. And sometimes, they need to be listened to. That's where you come. You listen to them. Even the most intimate secrets are told sometimes. This exchanging of secrets can only be done when you feel safe sharing them with a person. A friend buries your secrets within themselves.

6. Good Memories

Even the most boring party can take a 360 degree turn when you are with your friend. Times like these call for good memories. It would help if you shared loads of good memories. Even when time passes by, a bad day can make an excellent future memory.

Conclusion

It takes a lot of time, care and love to form a strong bond of friendship. We have to give it our best to keep that bond in good condition. Friends are precious to us, and we should make them feel likewise. And with the right person, friendship can last a lifetime.

Chapter 7:

6 Signs You Are Emotionally Unavailable

In times of need, all we want is emotional comfort. The people around us mainly provide it. But the question is, will we support them if the need arises? You might be emotionally unavailable for them when they need you. It is necessary to have some emotional stability to form some strong bonds. If you are emotionally unapproachable, you will have fewer friends than someone you stand mentally tall. It is not harmful to be emotionally unavailable, but you need to change that in the long run. And for that, you need to reflect on yourself first.

It would help if you always were your top priority. While knowing why you are emotionally unapproachable, you need to focus on yourself calmly. Giving respect and talking is not enough for someone to rely on you. You need to support them whenever needed. Talk your mind with them. Be honest with them. But not in a rude way, in a comforting way. So, next time they will come to you for emotional support and comfort. If you are relating to all these things, then here are some signs that confirm it.

1. You Keep People At A Distance

It is usual for an emotionally unavailable person to be seen alone at times. They tend to stay aloof at times; that way, they don't have to be emotionally available. And even if you meet people, you always find it challenging to make a bond with them. You might have a few friends and family members close to you. But you always find meeting new people an emotionally draining activity. You also might like to hang out with people, but opening up is not your forte. If you are emotionally unavailable, then you keep people at a hands distance from you.

2. You Have Insecurities

If you struggle to love yourself, then count it as a sign of emotional stress. People are likely to be unavailable emotionally for others when they are emotionally unavailable for themselves too. We always doubt the people who love us. How can they when I, myself, can't? And this self-hatred eventually results in a distant relationship with your fellow beings. Pampering yourself time by time is essential for every single one of us. It teaches us how one should be taken care of and how to support each other.

3. You Have A Terrible Past Experience

This could be one of the reasons for your unapproachable nature towards people. When you keep some terrible memory or trauma stored inside of you, it's most likely you cannot comfort some other being. It won't seem like something you would do. Because you keep this emotional difference, you become distant and are forced to live with those memories, making things worse. It would help if you talked things out. Either your parents or your friends. Tell them whatever is on your mind, and you will feel light at heart. Nothing can change the past once it's gone, but we can work on the future.

4. You Got Heartbroken

In most cases, people are not born with this nature to be emotionally unavailable. It often comes with heartbreak. If you had a breakup with your partner, that could affect your emotional life significantly. And if it was a long-term relationship, then you got emotionally deprived. But on the plus side, you got single again. Ready to choose from scratch. Instead, you look towards all the negative points of this breakup. Who knows, maybe you'll find someone better.

5. You Are An Introvert

Do you hate going to parties or gatherings? Does meeting with friends sound tiresome? If yes, then surprise, you are an introvert. Social life can be a mess sometimes. Sometimes we prefer a book to a person. That trait of ours makes us emotionally unavailable for others. It is not a bad thing to stay at home on a Friday night, but going out once in a while may be healthy for you. And the easiest way to do that is to make an extrovert friend. Then you won't need to make an effort. Everything will go smoothly.

6. You Hate Asking For Help

Do you feel so independent that you hate asking for help from others? Sometimes when we get support from others, we feel like they did a favor for us. So, instead of asking for help, we prefer to do everything alone, by ourselves. Asking for aid, from superior or inferior, is no big deal. Everyone needs help sometimes.

Conclusion

Being emotionally unavailable doesn't make you a wrong person, but being there for others gives us self-comfort too. It's not all bad to interact with others; instead, it's pretty fun if you try. It will make your life much easier, and you will have a lot of support too.

Chapter 8:
6 Lessons You Can Learn From A Breakup

Have you ever been in a relationship, and it hasn't ended well? Breakups may make you feel insecure about yourself; if your significant other has broken up with you, you might feel rejected. Although watching tv shows and eating a tub of ice cream may sound like the only logical thing to do after a breakup, it is the time to focus on yourself and see what went wrong in your previous relationship. Relationships teach us who exactly we are, it tells us what kind of people we want to love. Here are a few lessons you can learn from a breakup.

1. Happiness Comes From Within

At the start of a relationship, we all feel excited and beyond happy, but happiness is not true happiness. Happiness comes from within. This means that we don't want to have anyone else in our life to feel happy. Sure, you would feel lonely after a breakup, but time heals everything. When you are with someone who doesn't treat you the way you should be treated, then you might've forgotten your self-worth. You need to remember that you were not born with this person; this relationship was just a part of your life. You need to start loving yourself, start accepting that this is the way you are. Once you start believing that only you can make yourself truly happy, you will finally understand the true meaning of happiness.

2. It's About Us

Breakup helps you to understand that it was never about them; it was always about you. When going through a breakup, people often blame everything on their significant other, but it is not always about them. Breakup gives you space for your personal growth. A breakup is very enlightening, although it may bring out some insecurities but as soon as you tackle your inner demons, you realize that it is all about you.

3. You Can't Change Anyone

Haven't we all heard someone saying that we will change them? It may sound effortless trying to change someone's habits, but it is pretty impossible in reality. We cannot change someone unless that person also wants to change. Change comes from within, and not even your love can change your partner. If you and your partner broke up, it probably was for the best even though opposites attract, but too many differences can cause many problems. It is time to accept the fact that you need to find someone who satisfies your needs.

4. Believe In Your Gut

When something isn't right or the way it should be, we all feel about it; it can be our instincts warning us. Listen to your gut. Often, we tend to ignore what our gut is telling us, and we carry on like everything is fine when it is the opposite. Sometimes, your gut tells you that this is not the one, but ignoring it will lead to a bad breakup. So always listen to what your gut has to say; it's just your heart telling you what it wants.

5. Figure Out What Your Heart Truly Wants

When we go through a breakup, we all know it happened for a reason; there was something about that relationship that you didn't want. Now is the time to figure out what you want from a relationship. It is the time to focus on yourself, understand your emotional needs, and how you want a relationship to be. It is time to figure out what kind of a relationship you want. Once you figure this out, you know what you do and what you don't want from a relationship.

6. It Is Okay To Be Alone

After a breakup, some people feel abandoned as if they are all alone now, and they feel like it is not a good thing, but in reality, it is okay to be alone; you don't always need to be with someone. When you realize that you can make yourself happy and you don't want anyone else to do that, it is the time when you need to become selfish and think about yourself. Set some goals, achieve them, and don't just throw yourself into another relationship without figuring out what you truly want because it may just end up in heartbreak.

Conclusion

Breakups are hard to go through, but they happen for a reason; try to figure out what indeed went wrong. What you want from a relationship and remember it is okay to be alone; you don't need someone else to make you feel happy. You are enough for yourself.

Chapter 9:
6 Signs Your Love Is One Sided

While some things are better one-sided, like your favorite ice-cream cone that you don't want to share, your high school diary that knows all your enemies and crushes, and a game of solitaire. But a healthy relationship? Now that should be a two-sided situation. Unfortunately, when you're stuck in a one-sided relationship, it becomes easy to fool yourself every day that what you are experiencing is normal, when in reality, it could actually be toxic or even unworthy and loveless.

They could physically be sitting next to you, but you will find yourself being alone because of your emotional needs not being taken care of. Even though you have committed yourself to your partner, there's a fundamental difference between being selfless in love and giving it all without receiving anything at all. It might be possible that you're in denial, but the below signs of your one-sided love are hard to ignore.

1. **You're Constantly Second-Guessing Yourself**

If you don't get enough reassurance from your partner and constantly wonder if you are pretty enough, or intelligent enough, or funny enough, and always trying to live up to your partner's expectations, then you're definitely in a one-sided relationship. You tend to focus all of your energy and attention on being liked instead of being your true self and nurtured by your partner. It would be best if you always were your authentic self so the people who genuinely deserve you can get attracted to you and get relationships that match the true you.

2. You Apologize More Than Needed

Everyone makes mistakes. We are not some divine creatures who are all perfect and have no flaws. Sometimes you're at fault, sometimes your partner is. But if you end up saying sorry every single time, even if you had no idea about the fight, then maybe take a deeper look at your relationship. You may think that you're saving your relationship by doing this, but trust me, this is a very unhealthy sign. Cori Dixon-Fyle, founder and psychotherapist at Thriving Path, says, "Avoiding conflict results in dismissing your feelings." Solving fights should always be a team approach and not just one person's responsibility.

3. You're Always Making Excuses For Your Partner

Playing defense is excellent, but only on a soccer team. Suppose you are doing it constantly for your partner and justifying their behaviors to your circle of friends, family, and work colleagues. In that case, you're overlooking something that they are most likely seeing. If the people in your life are constantly alarming you, then maybe you should focus on your partner and see where the signs are coming from.

4. You Feel Insecure About Your Relationship

If you are never indeed at ease with your partner and often question the status of your relationship, then it's a clear sign that you are in a one-sided relationship. If you focus more on analyzing yourself, becoming more alluring, and choosing words or outfits that will keep your partner desiring you, then it's a major red flag. To feel unsettled and all-consumed in a relationship is not only exhausting, but it's also sustainable. Feeling constantly depleted in your relationship is also a sign that it's one-sided.

5. You're Giving Too Much

Giving too much and expecting just a little can never work in the long run. Suppose you're the only one in the relationship who makes all the plans. Do all the chores, remember all the important dates and events, consider stopping or making your partner realize that they aren't giving much in the relationship. Often when people give, they have some expectations in the back of their mind that the giving will be returned, but things fall apart when the other person never had those intentions. It's normal for a short while for one partner to carry the load more than the other; all relationships go through such stages, but constantly engaging in it is unhealthy.

6. You're Never Sure About How They Are Feeling

You can't read people's minds, nor are the communications transparent; you may end up overthinking their behaviors towards you and may be confused about how they're truly feeling. This uncertainty would cause you to dismiss your feelings in favor of thinking about them. This connection may be filled with guessing and speculations rather than knowing reality and seeing where they genuinely stand.

Conclusion

The best way to fix a one-sided relationship is to step away and focus on your self-worth and self-growth instead of trying to water a dead plant. You must focus on flourishing your own life instead of shifting your all to your partner. Your mental health should be your priority.

Love That Lasts

www.ingramcontent.com/pod-product-compliance
Lightning Source LLC
Chambersburg PA
CBHW071524080526
44588CB00011B/1556